AN EASTER HUNT

A Hide-and-Seek Story

Written by Sarah Reid Chisholm
Illustrated by Michelle Neavill

Augsburg
MINNEAPOLIS

Praise be to the God and Father of our Lord Jesus Christ! In his great mercy he has given us new birth into a living hope through the resurrection of Jesus Christ from the dead.

—1 Peter 1:3

AN EASTER HUNT
A Hide-and-Seek Story

Scripture is taken from the Holy Bible, New International Version, copyright © 1973, 1978, 1984 by the International Bible Society. Used by permission of Zondervan Bible Publishers.

ISBN 0-8066-2740-9   LCCN 94-72211

Manufactured in the U.S.A.   AF 9-2740

98   97   96   95   94   1   2   3   4   5   6   7   8   9   10

For my husband, Alex
S.R.C.

For Mom and Dad
M.L.N.

My mom whistled while she
picked daffodils in her
garden. "I love Easter," she
said with a big smile.

"What's so special about
Easter?" I asked.

"Is it special when
someone sticks up for you
even though they know
your mistakes?" she asked
me. "Is it special when one
person gives his life to help
another person?"

"Uh huh," I replied.

"Is it special to know that God loves you and has made you his child?"

"Yup," I said.

At Easter we celebrate these things," said Mom. "Jesus stuck up for us by giving his life so that we could be God's children. I have an idea. Let's have a special Easter hunt."

Instead of hiding Easter eggs or candy, Mom hid different things that would teach us something about Jesus' last few days on earth.

First Mom hid a wooden donkey in our living room. She explained that Jesus rode on a donkey into the big city of Jerusalem. People praised him and called him king.

Blessed is the king who comes in the name of the Lord.
—Luke 19:38

"Now hunt in the back yard for a blue doll table," Mom said.

She had us look for a table, because Jesus knocked over tables in the temple. He was angry that men were selling animals and cheating people out of money.

"How dare you turn my Father's house into a market!"
—John 2:15

Mom told us about a woman who poured some nice-smelling stuff on Jesus' head because she loved him. Jesus said the woman would always be remembered for that. So Mom hid a bottle of perfume in the kitchen.

"She has done a beautiful thing to me."
—Matthew 26:10

Next we had to find two chocolate hearts. The hearts taught us about the most important rules of all. Jesus said, "Love God with all your HEART, with all your soul and with all your mind." Jesus said we should love other people, too.

"There is no greater commandment than these."
—Mark 12:30

I'm glad there were two candy hearts so my brother and I each got one to eat.

Then we ran to the front yard to find my brother's stinky old red shoe. The shoe was supposed to help us remember a story about Jesus and dirty feet.

Before eating dinner with his disciples, Jesus washed their feet. Jesus told his disciples to follow his example and serve each other.

"Lord, are you going to wash my feet?"
—John 13:6

Mom put a can of olives in my brother's bedroom. Jesus prayed in a garden of olive trees. He asked God to help him because he knew the next day would not be easy.

He fell to the ground and prayed.
—Mark 14:35

The next day Jesus was arrested. It's hard to believe that some men hated Jesus and wanted to kill him. But it's true. Judas was one of Jesus' disciples. Judas led these men to Jesus so they could arrest him. They paid Judas 30 silver coins for snitching on Jesus.

So we looked near the garage for a small leather bag with 30 pennies in it.

"What are you willing to give me if I hand him over to you?"
—Matthew 26:15

Mom took the rooster from my farm animals and hid it in her bedroom. She told us about Peter, another one of Jesus' disciples.

After Jesus was arrested, Peter told three people that he didn't know Jesus. Peter lied because he didn't want to be arrested too. A rooster crowed right after Peter's third lie. Peter felt bad that he pretended he wasn't Jesus' friend.

"I don't know him,"
he said.
—Luke 22:57

Mom tied two sticks
together with string and
made a cross for us to find.
Jesus died hanging on a
cross of wood.

*"Surely he was the Son
of God!"*
—Matthew 27:54

Jesus' friends were very sad after he died. So Mom drew a sad face and put it in our dining room.

"Woman, why are you crying?"
—John 20:15

Jesus' body was put in a cave and the door was blocked with a big stone. That was called a tomb.

On Easter morning we had to look for a tomb that Mom made out of clay. It was easy to find. She put grass and flowers around it and placed it right in our backyard.

I ran over to the tomb and pushed the stone out of the way. "Jesus isn't there," I said.

"That's right," said my mom. "Jesus didn't stay in the tomb because God made him alive again. His disciples were so happy when they saw Jesus again. Jesus is alive and that is what Easter is all about."

*"He is not here; he
  has risen!"*
  —Luke 24:6

THE END